Here Is the Tropical Rain Forest

Madeleine Dunphy

ILLUSTRATED BY

Michael Rothman

Children's School

Web of Life
CHILDREN'S BOOKS

*H*ere is the tropical rain forest.

_H_*ere is the rain*

that drizzles and pours

and may fall every day

in this lush and wet world:

Here is the tropical rain forest.

*H*ere is the frog

who bathes in the rain

that drizzles and pours

and may fall every day

in this lush and wet world:

Here is the tropical rain forest.

*H*ere *is the bromeliad*

that shelters the frog

who bathes in the rain

that drizzles and pours

and may fall every day

in this lush and wet world:

Here is the tropical rain forest.

*H*ere is the tree,

which holds the bromeliad

that shelters the frog

who bathes in the rain

that drizzles and pours

and may fall every day

in this lush and wet world:

Here is the tropical rain forest.

*H*ere is the sloth

that hangs from the tree,

which holds the bromeliad

that shelters the frog

who bathes in the rain

that drizzles and pours

and may fall every day

in this lush and wet world:

Here is the tropical rain forest.

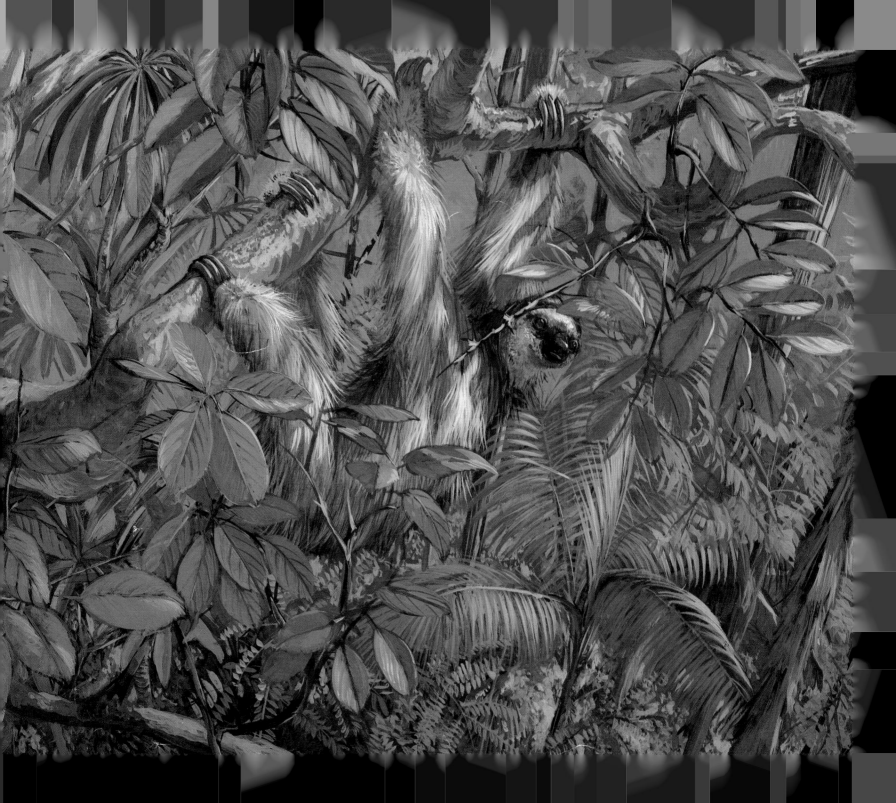

*H*ere is the eagle

who hunts the sloth

that hangs from the tree,

which holds the bromeliad

that shelters the frog

who bathes in the rain

that drizzles and pours

and may fall every day

in this lush and wet world:

Here is the tropical rain forest.

Here are the monkeys

that flee from the eagle

who hunts the sloth

that hangs from the tree,

which holds the bromeliad

that shelters the frog

who bathes in the rain

that drizzles and pours

and may fall every day

in this lush and wet world:

Here is the tropical rain forest.

*H*ere are the figs,

which are dropped by the monkeys

that flee from the eagle

who hunts the sloth

that hangs from the tree,

which holds the bromeliad

that shelters the frog

who bathes in the rain

that drizzles and pours

and may fall every day

in this lush and wet world:

Here is the tropical rain forest.

Here are the peccaries

that eat the figs,

which are dropped by the monkeys

that flee from the eagle

who hunts the sloth

that hangs from the tree,

which holds the bromeliad

that shelters the frog

who bathes in the rain

that drizzles and pours

and may fall every day

in this lush and wet world:

Here is the tropical rain forest.

*H*ere is the jaguar

who stalks the peccaries

that eat the figs,

which are dropped by the monkeys

that flee from the eagle

who hunts the sloth

that hangs from the tree,

which holds the bromeliad

that shelters the frog

who bathes in the rain

that drizzles and pours

and may fall every day

in this lush and wet world:

Here is the tropical rain forest.

*H*ere is the caiman

that fights the jaguar

who stalks the peccaries

that eat the figs,

which are dropped by the monkeys

that flee from the eagle

who hunts the sloth

that hangs from the tree,

which holds the bromeliad

that shelters the frog

who bathes in the rain

that drizzles and pours

and may fall every day

in this lush and wet world:

Here is the tropical rain forest.

*H*ere is the river,

which is home to the caiman

that fights the jaguar

who stalks the peccaries

that eat the figs,

which are dropped by the monkeys

that flee from the eagle

who hunts the sloth

that hangs from the tree,

which holds the bromeliad

that shelters the frog

who bathes in the rain

that drizzles and pours

and may fall every day

in this lush and wet world:

Here is the tropical rain forest.

*H*ere is the rain

that fills the river,

which is home to the caiman

that fights the jaguar

who stalks the peccaries

that eat the figs,

which are dropped by the monkeys

that flee from the eagle

who hunts the sloth

that hangs from the tree,

which holds the bromeliad

that shelters the frog

who bathes in the rain

that drizzles and pours

and may fall every day

in this lush and wet world:

Here is the tropical rain forest.

Wildlife of the Tropical Rain Forest

THREE-TOED SLOTH

BLUNT-HEADED TREE SNAKE

RED-RUMPED AGOUTI

TOAD-HEADED TURTLE

COMMON CAIMAN

The animals and plants shown in this book live in the tropical rain forests of Central and South America. Tropical rain forests are the oldest and most complex ecosystems on land. They cover seven percent of the Earth's land surface, yet they contain over half of the world's animal and plant species.

They are called rain forests because of their heavy rainfall. Some rain forests receive as much as 400 inches of rain a year. Tropical rain forests are located in the tropics near the equator. Because of this, they are warm day and night, winter and summer. This lack of cool and dry seasons is one of the reasons life is so prolific in the rain forest.

Many of the foods we eat, such as bananas, cashews, chocolate, cinnamon, lemons, oranges, and papayas, originated in the rain forest. Additionally, many of the medicines

LITTLE HERMIT HUMMINGBIRD

DART ARROW FROG

HARPY EAGLE

BROWN CAPUCHIN MONKEY

JAGUAR

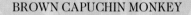

COLLARED PECCARY

we use owe their existence to rain forest plants.

Despite these many wonders, tropical rain forests are being cut down for logging, mining, cattle ranching, the building of dams, and other reasons. Scientists estimate that 50 million acres of tropical rain forest are lost each year, an area roughly equivalent to the states of New York, New Jersey, Massachusetts, and Connecticut combined. Countless animal and plant species become extinct each year due to this destruction.

We must act now to help ensure the survival of tropical rain forests. To find out what you can do, write to the Rainforest Alliance, 665 Broadway, Suite 500, New York, NY 10012, or check out their website at www.rainforest-alliance.org.

For my mother, Claire, who showed me the wonders of nature.
—M.D.

Much of the scientific material for this book is based on research by
Dr. Scott Mori and Carol Gracie of the New York Botanical Garden.
Many thanks for their support, encouragement, and friendship.
—M.R.

Text ©2006 by Madeleine Dunphy.
Illustrations ©2006 and © 1994 by Michael Rothman.

First published in hardcover in 1994 by Hyperion Books for Children.
First published in paperback in 1997 by Hyperion Paperbacks for Children.

For information, write to:
Web of Life Children's Books
P.O. Box 2726, Berkeley, California 94702

Published in the United States in 2006 by Web of Life Children's Books.

Printed in Singapore.

Cataloging-in-Publication Data is on file with the Library of Congress.

ISBN 0-9773795-0-7 (paperback edition)
978-0-9773795-0-7

ISBN 0-9773795-1-5 (hardcover edition)
978-0-9773795-1-4

The artwork for this book was prepared using watercolor.

Read all the books in the series:
*Here Is the African Savanna, Here Is the Coral Reef, Here Is the Wetland,
Here Is the Southwestern Desert,* and *Here Is the Arctic Winter.*

For more information about our books, and the authors
and artists who create them, visit our website:
www.weboflifebooks.com

Distributed by Publishers Group West